Sherry's

CONSOMMÉ

A Collection of Wise Tales and Lessons

SHERRY DAVIS

SHERRY'S CONSOMMÉ

© Copyright 2023 By Sherry Davis

All rights reserved.

Dedication

I will say of the Lord, He is my refuge and my fortress: my God; in him will I trust. **Psalms 91:2**

I gladly give God praises for all he has done in my life. My lord and Savior Jesus Christ gave me encouragement throughout my life when I felt totally alone. In my opinion, I think a lot of people go through a time in their life where they fell there is no hope and that's maybe why they take up with the use of alcohol or drugs to comfort their hearts. My life goal is to be happy, loved, and have a peace of mind. I learned during my trails of life that being happy comes from within, and knowing God is a comforter. I still find joy when am riding my bike and taking long walks. In my opinion, what takes away one's happiness is trying to allow someone else to be responsible for your happiness which is a great mistake.

Now when it comes to love, I learned to love myself. Doing things with others that make me happy. Doing things by myself that makes you happy, however there was a time I did not know how to love myself because of life situations. I learned through God that my mental well-being and being positive helped me love myself and to have a peaceful mindset.

I am also thankful for my entire family who I love so much. I could say a lot of things individually about my large family however, I will share more about them in another book. I just love them all.

O give thanks unto the Lord; for he is good; for his mercy endureth forever. **1 Chronicles 16:34**

Table of Contents

ONE

Not a Competition, It Is a Service

I returned and saw under the sun, that the race is not to the swift, nor the battle to the strong, neither yet bread to the wise, nor yet riches to men of understanding, nor yet favour to men of skill; but time and chance happeneth to them all. **Ecclesiastes 9:11**

If you knew me as a child, you would have seen a young girl that liked to listen to music, dancing, and riding her bike and most importantly stay away from confusion.

Staying in my safe space made me look antisocial yet I was reserving my peace. Things I was taught as a child has help me during my adulthood. As a leader I would study my agenda for the next day to ensure clarity on the subjects. I could not prepare for the unknown, but I kept a prayer in my heart. I have never wanted to be a person to be in the spotlight because of the attention it brings. I like being to myself and securing my privacy. Somehow when I get around kind and caring people, I am asked to make a difference by helping others and I give in to the request to serve. One example is when I was asked to be a basketball coach with the police department. The police officers from the West Precinct came to the school and convinced me to coach girls' basketball in the Ensley community. Amazingly, I learned a lot about coaching from a former NFL football player and some great parent volunteers.

Then I was elected by local members to serve as president of our education association. Next, I was elected as a leader to state and national association positions. Each position to serve was by request of someone who supported me after I accepted the challenge. On a state level God sent wonderful support through at that time, EPPP Manager Dr. Tyna Davis who was also a former State Association President. She asked me, "What do you know about technology?" I shared with her the programs I used at the school, and she submitted my name for a program called NPP with the National Education Association. The NPP team created lots of great programs for the members. I traveled to California, Chicago, and Washington D.C. many times with that program. That assignment allowed me to have a brief face to face visit with family members who lived in those cities during my travels. We learned in one of my leadership training that staying connected with family is essential. That assignment was the beginning of my long-term service to members on a national level. Dr. Davis has a wealth of knowledge, and her guidance is unmeasurable. Her support during my leadership as state president will always be treasured. Dr. Tyna Davis has been a mentor to many individuals who reaches out to her. She is a Phenomenal woman.

On a national level I had a guardian earthly angel who is now the National Education President, Mrs. Becky Pringle. She placed me on committees where I was truly like a fish out of water when I started, but by the end I was able to articulate knowledgeably about the subjects in which I was a participant. There is also kind-heartedness Princess Moss who is now the Vice President of the National Education Association. Princess came through Alabama while heading to a national meeting and checked on me along with former Executive Director John Stocks of The National Education Association. Their visit gave the encouragement I needed at that time to keep moving forward.

Then there was the former President of the National Education Association Reg Weaver and former Alabama Education Association, Associate Executive Director, Dr. Joe Reed. Both men were filled with knowledge of both organizations and would impart positive ways to lead members without confusion. Both former leaders reminded me that my leadership was for the members and not personal. All those positions were requests of members, and they truly took me out of my comfort zone. I learned once I was in these positions, I had to keep moving forward to run the race that was set before me. Moving Forward became my theme. There were lots of members who showed their support by sending encouraging words and praying to keep me focus on things that matter. What I learned in leadership is, no true leader has all the answers. Staying positive made me stay close to God.

One Sunday I was encouraged to go before the alter for prayer while Bishop Bender was praying for the members. Once he finished praying, he said it is done. I have strong faith, but I was not sure if I wanted to continue in that position because of the high level of stress that came with it. There were other churches in Birmingham that had put up my flyer for re-election in their churches which blew my mind that the churches stepped up and supported me. I was surprised when I won reelection. My mind went back to the bishop's prayer, and I knew it was in God's will for me to serve in the position as president a second term. I had to tell those pastors and all supporters/educators thank you for all their help. I thank God for the abundance of spiritual help He sent during my entire leadership terms.

Those positions took me out of my comfort zone but allowed me to service.

Competing sometimes bring about confusion. Confusion can be defined as a lack of understanding. I learn it is important to run for the position and not against the other candidate(s). When there are big or small elections sometimes the competition causes a dispute in the results. Most of the time others cause issues because they believe their way is always right and they are competing for some type of acknowledgement.

I learned in my last studies about Conflict Resolution. In conflict resolution there should be a win-win resolution however it cannot be if the information being discussed is not equal/fair/honest, or the individuals involved do not want to share the outcome. As for competing it is a complicated issue because it brings stress which sometimes creates enemies. I never thought of my service in leadership as a race or competition or to be better than others but to help others achieve their goals through my service to them.

For God is not the author of confusion, but of peace, as in all churches of the saints. **1 Corinthians 14:33**

T W O

Delay and Not Denied

The Lord is nigh unto them that are of a broken heart; and saveth such as be of a contrite spirit. **Psalms 34:18**

Delayed in not denied, is a common term that is used by many however for me, it was a fact.

The issues I have gone through throughout the years, guided my life lessons. I realized that all the no's that I got when I applied for some jobs, when I asked for help, and when I was denied being in certain circles was only a delay. The other thing that was delayed that meant a lot for me was college. I never told my mother what the guy at in the government office was trying to do to me, so I decided to drop out of college. He was the case manager assigned to our family case and if I stayed in school my stepfather's benefits would have paid for my college up to the age of 24. I was right out of high school. My mother was so upset but she did not know that the case manager continuously was calling me at our home making unwanted advances to me. I figured I would just stop going to college altogether so that I would not have to put up with his advances. That situation caused a lot of bad feeling within me because I didn't know how to deal with it without causing issues with my mother and her husband's income being affected. My stepfather was an honorably discharged veteran who had suffered a stroke and that was the source of income for the entire family. I kindly told the caseworker no to his unwanted advances and I never went back to his office again. I have a problem with men that prey on women in that way, for I personally believe they are cowards.

As for the jobs, God gave me longevity in the education system. I learned that my help comes from the Lord. He is a way maker. As for social circles I learned that all social groups do not promote positive service however the social service circles I am a part of are positive. As of this day I have earned an associate's, bachelors, masters, and an advance certificate in Conflict Resolution on the doctoral level without completing the dissertation. I lost my motivation to complete my doctorate once my mother died.

College was delayed but not totally denied.

A soft answer turneth away wrath: but grievous words stir up anger. **Proverbs 15:1.**

THREE

Not a Competition, It Is a Service

When I was a child, I spake as a child, I understood as a child, I thought as a child: but when I became a man, I put away childish things. **I Corinthians 13:11**

As a child, I reflected on being an adult as many children do. When I became an adult, I reflected on the fun things that happen as a child. It's funny because the mind is always coming and going through reflections of the past. I have so many fond memories of my grandparents who lived in West Alabama. The town in West Alabama is very small. The US census stated in 2021 there was less than 1000 people in that Township.

My maternal grandparents in West Alabama made life comfortable for us when I visited, and they had such an abundance of food at home. Eating out was not the norm. My grandfather Sam Cunningham really loved my grandmother Lizzie Estes Cunningham. My mother Hilda told me a beautiful story about her father and mother. She said her mother loved bacon and, in those days, when she was growing up, they did not have a lot of money. She said her father worked a whole day to earn money just to buy her mother her bacon. Well by the time I got to be a little girl my grandfather had a smokehouse for the family, and it was filled with pork. My grandmother had a garden where she grew peanuts and sweet potatoes. My grandmother passed away when I was about seven years old. I can remember walking into the smokehouse with my sisters when they would go to get selected smoked pork for dinner. In my grandfather's freezer he had a variety of cut beef. His community was very close. When one of his neighbors would slaughter a cow and my grandfather slaughtered a pig, they would trade half of their slaughtered meat with one another. My grandparents had chickens in the yard (free range during the day) for eggs and meals. During Christmas there were large apples, oranges, nuts, and lots of homemade cakes and pies. Also, a fresh cut Christmas tree sat in the living room.

My siblings were/are Barbara and Brenda and my brother Bobby who was the oldest. They lived with my grandparents. My grandparents gave my mother the opportunity to restart her life once she was divorced from their father who was much older than her. My sisters became mother's babysitters in summer because they were teenagers when I was younger. In the rural area in the 60s my grandparents didn't have indoor plumbing, but they did have a running water faucet outside. My sisters would pull my bath together outside in the front yard in the summertime when I had to visit. Both were hilarious. The bath outside in the front yard was embarrassing to me, but it was the way of life there. They would have had to bring the palls of water into the house and fill the tin tub then use the same process to empty the tin tub. The funny part about those days are Barbara asked how I can remember these things being I was very young. I told her I remember everything.

Somethings I cannot forget because family always reminded me of things that I may have gotten into as a little girl. One thing I remember for sure with my grandmother Lizzie was she loved to go fishing. Her sister in Mississippi had a fishing pond on her property which started her love for fishing. This fishing trip happen in Alabama on a sunny day. I was not school age. One day as we were walking back home, I picked an apple off the tree. I always would get a fruit off a tree because there was various fruit in our path (apple, figs, peach, and pear). As we walked my grandmother stopped at one of her friend homes to chit-chat for a while. As we sat inside the neighbor's house my grandmother asked me for a bite of my apple. I said no. Let me share some background as to why I said no. Those among us who are aware of people that dip snuff needs to know my grandmother was a snuff dipper. She grabbed the apple and took a bite out of it. I walked to the front door of her friend's home and threw the apple out the door. My grandmother said to me, "Now you don't have an apple!" She said, I needed to learn to share. The problem was not sharing, the problem was the snuff. That brown snuff in my opinion as a child, was gross. I did learn to share and how to proportion my giving. That was a life lesson.

Having to stay with my grandparents and my siblings when school was out was different than the big city life. Before we talk about the big city, I must mention this about my father. He was raised by two caucasian ladies who were related to my father's father. My mother told me that her mother-in-law, Ella Tucker Davis Williams (my paternal grandmother) moved in with her for a while before she left and went back east. Grandmother Ella was a jolly person whose laughter was memorable. She was born in Washington DC. She grew up in Virginia. Her last years of life were spent traveling from income that was residual from her family's inheritance according to my first cousin Tim Williams who passed away some years ago in New York. His mother aunt Elizabeth looked a lot like my oldest daughter. She had long hair with a beautiful shape. Tim was going to share more information on our grandmother, but he passed away suddenly before we could get together. Our Grandmother lived with them a few years once she became sickly there in New York.

I had to spend one week out of my summer with my father and his wife. This was the divorce agreement. John Davis and his wife had no children, but she had nephews and nieces that she helped take care of who lived with them from time to time. The times I stayed with them seems to have been longer than a week (in a child's mind). My father's wife was a public-school teacher in a different part of West Alabama, it was in the same town granddaddy Sam was born. I would spend my days assisting her with her summer school class. The evenings were worse in my opinion because they were spent shucking corn and shelling purple hull peas for the winter. The purple on my fingers would take days to remove. I would be packed and ready to go when my grandfather and brother came and got me to take me to his home. Once I became a teenager those summer days changed, and I did not need a sitter anymore. As I got older, I did not visit West Alabama as much because the country life compared to the city life is no way the same.

As of this day I have a sister and other family members who live in West Alabama who are comfortable with their lifestyle. Not saying that the city life is great, but it is comfortable here in the South. My first cousin Sharon who I love lives in West Alabama, told me a few years ago that she prays for me often. I asked her why and she said that she knows that city life can dangerous. There are stories about Sharon and me. We won't tell anyone all the other stories but this one I can tell. We went to Mississippi to a place to dance as teenagers. This place was in a field. The inside of the building was amazing. We were given a ticket for food once we paid upon entering the building. The smell of fried fish could be smelled once you got into the building. There were two floors. The D.J. who was on a local station in Birmingham was in the center of the floors on the back wall. I do not remember dancing, but I do remember sitting on the second floor enjoying the whiting fish sandwich while watching everyone else on the first floor. Sharon is very quiet. She does not do a lot of talking and she has a gentle spirit. We are so much alike as it relates to quiet and being in a peaceful mindset.

I remembered praying and asking God to watch over my oldest daughter Toy who moved out of town to work two years in Tennessee, Louisiana, and Texas. My first cousin Gwendolyn stepped in and allowed her to stay with her until she could find a safe neighborhood that she was comfortable living in Tennessee. Sharon, Gwendolyn, and I were very close as children until our mothers took us to different cities, but our love as first cousins never changed. Sharon and Gwendolyn's fathers (John and Charles) are my mother's two younger brother's oldest children. They are still my first best friends. My family is a close-knit group who love each other unconditionally. We do not have to talk to one another daily because our hearts were mended together as children.

Let's talk about the city life. I attend church daycare, elementary, and high school in Birmingham Alabama. As youth we walked to places together such as school and downtown. Walking downtown was faster that taking the bus. We lived in walking distance of the area where many civil rights events happened. Most of us attended schools in our own community. I attended one of the first high schools for people of color in this city. Educators at the school instilled pride and confidence in the students and respect for the community. Many of the professional educators lived right there in the community. The colors purple and white are our high school colors were respected and required for students to wear when attending sports related events and during the pep rally. The proper name of the school is Arthur Harold Parker High School in the Smithfield community. I was excited like all the other young elementary school children to be going to the great big school sitting on 8th Avenue in Smithfield. I was also looking forward to lunch because one of my childhood friends Bernadette, older sisters would bring her their cake from the lunchroom. The slice of cake was so large that she would share it with Myrtle and I. Lunch was always good, even though I took a lunch most days because of my finicky ways, but I did purchase a slice of cake when I wanted a slice. I did not know the value of such a prestigious school when I was growing up. Parker High school has been a positive part of developing educators, attorneys, judges, doctors, professionals, famous actors, athletics, and great friendships from within those walls. The current administrator and educators call the Parker "The

University". Overall, I appreciate the history of this magnificent school now more since becoming an adult.

There is nothing better for a man, than that he should eat and drink, and that he should make his soul enjoy good in his labour. This also I saw, that it was from the hand of God.

Ecclesiastes 2:24

FOUR

Manifest

When I was a child, I spake as a child, I understood as a child, I thought as a child: but when I became a man, I put away childish things. **I Corinthians 13:11**

My definition of manifest as it relates to me is a clear statement or action of what I want and believing I will receive it.

Let me share with you the things that I wanted in life. I wanted a college degree, so I achieved that mission, and it became a great reality. I achieve several college degrees. Another manifestation that I wanted that came to pass was to meet some of my mother's family in Mississippi. My mother Hilda passed away in April of 2013. I realize when I saw her birth certificate that she had never taken me to her hometown where she grew up as a little girl. In 2019 I visited my mother's maternal aunt Sylvia who at that time was 104 years old. She was in her right mind. She also remembered each one of her five brothers and five sisters. Yes, there was 11 of them. She remembered her mother's name (Daisy Shumpert Estes) and her father's name (Raf

Estes). She remembered my grandmother's beautiful long hair. She remembered my grandparent's names and all their children. She even remembered the girl child that died as a baby/toddler. My mother use to tell me about the baby sister who died and how it broke my grandmother's heart. Aunt Sylvia reminisce on how my grandfather used call out one of his son's names all the time because he stayed into something all the time. It was Uncle Boogie (John). My great aunt was right because my mother used to call out his name all the time too as an adult. My uncle would get into stuff as an adult, and he would laugh his way through the whole issue. He was a good uncle. My mother was the oldest of her parent's children and the four boys were younger than her. My great aunt asked me did I complete high school and I replied yes. She said to me, "I did too." For those that don't know the history in the South namely Mississippi, everyone did not get to go to school in those day. I began to research my mother's family history when she died. The records in the U.S. Census and other documents show that only certain children in the family were allowed to attend school in that state. My great aunt was one of them that had the opportunity and so did my grandmother. One of my mother's first cousin in Mississippi who is the same age I am said she had to leave school and work in the field to help her father with his crops and could not finish school.

What a privilege it is to have public schools for all children no matter their zip code, race, or gender.

The other manifestation that I made, was to be a good mother. My children were almost two years apart and they were very active in arts from middle school to college. I was that mother that had children in three different public schools at once. The easiest year I had, as it relates to the arts, was when all three were participating in the Christmas musical at the Boutwell Auditorium. That was one event, and all schools were in the same place. The most complicated year was having to drive to two different high schools (Jackson-Olin and Ramsay) on the same Sunday for choir concerts. The interesting year was when Calvin III song with the choir, played with the band, and escorted the interim Superintendent the same night of the program at the Boutwell Auditorium. Here is the story that goes with my son's activities that night. His vocal music teacher called the school where I worked and voiced his opinion that my son should only sing. I asked the teacher, "What's wrong with the various roles?" He hung up on me. Two months later the same teacher called me and requested a bow tie and cummerbund to be made from Kente cloth. I politely asked when do you need them?

As for college they gave me a short break and attended the same HBCU, Alabama State University, in Montgomery, Alabama yet there was marching band, concert choir, and a beauty pageant. Although, it was only for a couple of years that they were at the same school together. I enjoyed them being at one school because they were able to support one another.

Not sure if that made me a good mother but I know in my heart it shows my children (Toy, Tam, and Calvin III) that I did my very best to allow them to participate in activities with their peers. Children need to know how to get along with others to be productive citizens in the community.

As a parent, I had to learn to speak, pray and manifest that my children would be safe in their everyday walk of life especially when they went off to college. As their mother I learned there were no set patterns for raising children and that each child was different. I had to love each one accordingly. I also believe that my relationship with my grandchildren (Chloe and Carmen) will be as close or closer as I have with my children. It is a day-to-day process because their generation has a love for technology. I appreciate my granddaughters because I know they really don't want to talk but they do like the funny texts I send them. I just want to keep the communication open and if sending a text is the way to communicate with today's youth, I will do it.

I learned in life that I had to declare and believe positive things will happen for my friends and family. I learned early in life that patience and prayer is a major part of the success. As I became older, I've began to speak things into my life that are positive. I cannot manifest or believe that things are going to happen if I do not put my faith in God. I have a journal where I write my beliefs, my manifestations, and declarations that helps empower my faith. When someone tells me I can't do something that I know God will grant my desire I don't listen to them. I know God can manifest the things I desire and need in my life. I told my adult children, if you want something, you must believe God can make it happen. Our children must be given a mindset to believe in God. It is imperative that they learn to live by faith so that they will be able to receive their earthly blessing from God.

Lo, children are an heritage from the Lord: and the fruit of the womb is his reward. **Psalms 127:3**

FIVE

Pushing forward

But the fruit of the spirit is love, joy, peace, long-suffering, gentleness, goodness, faith, meekness, temperance: against such there is no law.
Galatians 5:22-23

Many times, issues in my life have tried to keep me feeling hopeless. One thing for sure is when negative words that come out of individuals' mouth will make you feel discouraged. Most of the time this comes from people or individuals who are missing positive reinforcement in their own lives. As for myself I've learned to let the negative behavior from others push me forward.

When I pray God sends support to help me stand against the negative issues that I was facing. Forgiving others who may have treated me wrong helped move me into a positive level in my life. The hard part of test is forgetting the action that caused the pain from the negative behavior someone held against me.

As a leader I had to remember to keep moving forward. There's a spiritual and a natural part to moving forward. If I stop moving and exercising in the natural it causes issues with the body such as stiffness in parts of the body. In the spiritual we must keep growing in the word and exercising our faith in God.

During my retired life I've learned to keep busy. As I've gotten older, I also realized that I cannot do some of the things I used to, but I must find age-appropriate activities. Age-appropriate activities such as walking when I used to be able to run. The last time I went running with Tamara I thought I was going to have a heart attack. I couldn't catch my breath; however, it was hot that day. I realized that day I was getting too old to run in the sun.

It takes a combination of things to stay positive and to apply the fruits of the spirit in your life. I promise you the fruits of the spirit do not just come to you easily. It takes a little of each fruit of the spirit every day to stay positive. For some people it takes counting to 10 or 100 whichever time limit they need to calm down. For some others it takes walking away to calm down. Perfect example is how tempers and temperaments change during the pandemic with society on social media and in person. I was at the post office to check on my post office box like I have done once a month for at least 15 years. I noticed something strange was going with my box, there was no mail when I checked the box for weeks. I always went on weekends which meant the main office building was closed. I finally got a chance to go inside one day before it closed and asked what was going on with my mailbox. In the past years the ladies at the post office would call me and ask why I haven't come and cleared out my box because it had begun to get cluttered. This day the postal worker behind the counter became outraged when I asked why I did not have mail. He stated I should have kept my receipt and then I would have known the due date for renewal. He was very loud in his response. At that point I knew it was time to walk away because he was not having a good day. I went to another post office and got a new post office box and just so happen there was a regional supervisor there that handles those kinds of situations. He listened patiently to my ordeal that happened the previous day. I am thankful that I did not try to go back and forth with the employee.

And to knowledge temperance; and to temperance patience; and to patience godliness. **2 Peter 1:6**

SIX

Putting on Blinders

Blessed are the merciful: for they shall obtain mercy.
Matthew 5:7

Once I am visiting another country, I began to see people who were dressed differently than myself or what I thought was inappropriate. I began to judge these individuals and immediately the Lord began to deal with my mindset. It is so important to accept individuals as they are. That was a great lesson that I learned even though individuals constantly are judging me.

Working in a school I learned that children come as they are, and they dress according to their family income. When I began to work in the schools, I realized I had to put blinders on and listen to their hearts as they would talk to me. I learned also that my co-worker needed that same respect. No judgement. I can't work with people or serve people when I judge them unfairly. I learned that the people I was judging would be out of a negative observation. My position in this world is to overlook or put on blinders to not see how negative others are and use my positive energy on those who may need that energy.

Since I've gotten older, I've learned to respect people's differences. I learn that I cannot tell people what to wear no matter what I think about their choice. I learn that changes in individual's livelihood could cause them to dress different, eat different, and to act different.

Let's talk about people acting different. It's so important for me to stay humble. My daughter asked, how is it that people walk around with their nose up in the air as if they are better than everyone around them? I told her I never understood that myself. They get up, go to work every day, depend on their paycheck every week or whenever they get it, however they pretend they have a better social status. The worst part of it is, they treat others badly because they think they are better than their coworker who is making the same pay. I reminded my daughter that staying humble and true to herself is much better than pretending and mistreating others. Personally, I knew as a state national leader that I needed to stay grounded. I knew that my elected position was only temporary. I'm thankful for the experience however I knew that I needed to keep the same friendly attitude that I had before I became a leader. I knew that some of the people that showered me with kindness and attention would end once the position was over. Now the sincere people who were genuinely kind to me still shows love and kindness. The great thing is my friends and associates who were friends and associates are still my friends and associate and nothing ever changed. I made some decisions as a leader and yes people act different towards me because of the results. Did I feel good about the decisions I had to made? Yes, most of them.

People felt different about me when the outcomes did not favor them. As a leader I knew that I had to make decisions where sometimes both parties would be upset with me.

One thing we learn in studying Conflict Resolution is, there should be an even divider when it comes to trying to resolve conflict. So, if both parties ended up not liking the results it shows no favoritism was used, just facts in my opinion. The important thing is the issues were placed on the table and discussed. I remember during an internship in a law office, the attorney was mediating a case. The strange thing about the case was we knew something wasn't right about one of the parties involved in the mediation, but we had to put on blinders during that process and stay focused on coming to a solution. After two hours of negotiations to resolve their issues, the entire discussion fell apart. Once the attorney dismissed both parties, we debriefed in the conference room, and we agreed that we foresaw a possible issue brewing about midways of the negotiation.

I can do all things through Christ which strengthens me.
Philippians 4:13

SEVEN

Siblings

Train up a child in the way he should go: and when he is old, he will not depart from it. **Proverbs 22:6**

My siblings were older than myself. They were my babysitters, at least my sisters were when they were needed. When I would visit our grandparents. I had the privilege to be with all three of them. The most that I can remember about my brother is, he was humble and kind. He worked all the time and always had a pretty car. My brother had about two or three stories he liked to tell me about my grandmother. One of the stories was in reference to my love for climbing as a little girl. My grandmother had a China cabinet, in his words, grandmother Lizzie told me to get down and I kept climbing. As you would know the cabinet fell on top of me breaking all the dishes. My brother and my grandmother thought the unspeakable had happened to me. Bobby stated shortly after the cabinet fell, I came crawling from underneath the rubble. I was built tough from birth.

Another story that Bobby liked to tell is about how much I love ice cream. We went to the shopping area of town to pick up some groceries and I began to beg for ice cream. My grandmother told me it was too cold for ice cream. Well, she gave in to me and let me have the ice cream. As my grandmother, my brother and I began to walk back to the house my hands began to get cold from holding the ice cream. My brother who was the oldest of all of us, picked me up and put me on his shoulders and held my ice cream for me all the way back home.

Bobby would tell these stories like they happened yesterday, and he would be laughing as he tells them over and over. He was a good person and I think my grandfather did an excellent job raising him with his sons. Even though my uncles moved away and went to Cleveland, Bobby stayed there and supported my grandfather because he knew my grandfather needed his support.

My sisters were totally different. Barbara, she was on the quiet side, until she was with Brenda. Brenda had a way of bringing the fun out of everybody. Barbara would go along with whatever Brenda was getting ready to do until it conflicted with her. One day they went to the store and came back with a pint of black walnut ice cream. Brenda cut the ice cream in half with the knife right through the cartoon. Well, one side was bigger than the other side. They begin to argue. I was much younger than them, so I took a seat at the table and watched them exchange words. I also noticed the ice cream was melting. I grabbed the spoon, and I began to eat the ice cream. At some point they stopped arguing when they noticed I was eating up the ice cream.

Amazingly their entire attention turned to me just because I was trying to save that ice cream.

I had mixed emotions when they would come here to Birmingham to keep me because it would take them up until the last minute to pick me up from daycare at the church. It was located downtown in the church on the opposite corner from 16th Street Baptist Church. My sisters would be hanging out with their friends talking and laughing (being teenagers). I was the little person, so I had to walk behind them most of time. Walking behind them was the norm for this little sister. One day I was trailing behind them, and they had gotten a bag of chocolate covered nuts from one of the big department stores downtown. It was a happy day because I was holding a bag of chocolates. As they walked and talked, they noticed I was quiet and right in the middle of the street as we were crossing by the park where the Civil Rights building is now, they took the bag of candy. It might have been two or three pieces left. Then the show really started because I refused to move until they returned the bag of candy. Everybody knows you don't get fulfillment if you don't eat the last piece. They lifted me up by my arms in the air to get me across the street. They did not return the candy.

There is one other story that I would like to share about Brenda, Barbara, and firecrackers. I was young but I can remember this event so well because it brought fear into my heart. It was the 4th of July, and my sisters were throwing firecrackers at some of the neighbors, and they begin throwing them back at them. It seemed to have been a game that they played all the time on the 4th of July. I was standing on the front porch watching. At one point someone threw a cherry bomb and Brenda got hit in the face. She began to scream loud and was crying. There was not a lot of damage done and I think it might have just been more of the explosion heat and shock that frightened her. I have never purchased fireworks for this reason.

Barbara got married so she became a lot more mature and a mother. Brenda graduated from high school, and moved to Cleveland where four of my mother's brothers were living. I'm sure Cleveland, Ohio has a lot of Cunningham's family there. When Brenda returned to West Alabama, she married a soldier who was recently out of the military. They moved to Chicago where my mother had another brother (Samson) living there. Uncle Samson was a child from Sam's first marriage. Samson was born in Tuscaloosa, Alabama. His son Sandy became one of my best friends. He was a great first cousin up until his untimely death on his motorcycle. He and his father were great supporters of Brenda when she moved to Chicago. Brenda lived in Chicago for many years. I used to go stay with her during holidays and summers as a teenager as I did when she lived in West Alabama. I can remember Brenda going to work and telling me, "Do not go outside this house". Well, she didn't have any snacks. I made the choice to leave the apartment and crossed the dangerous street. I went to the store got me some snacks and came back at the apartment. When Brenda return home she stated, "I knew you was going to go out the apartment!". The fun part about taking orders from sisters is that they are sisters not mothers, so I had a little leave way to be mischievous in a good way. As my return home, Brenda took me on my first flight to Birmingham from Chicago. Brenda was very high class, and she said there was no way she was going to ride a bus to

Alabama. I had my first meal on the plane by to Alabama which was Cordon Bleu.

Brenda retired from Illinois Bell and came back to Alabama for a short period of time before she moved to Georgia. Once she moved to Georgia, she encouraged many of the young people in the family that wanted to leave West Alabama to come relocate to Georgia. I shall always remember; she was so happy as a teenager and young adult.

Brenda was this fun-loving person. She would play music all the time and say come on let's dance. I think I got my passion for having a great desserts from her. She would find the best cakes, pastries, and candies to share with everyone. I miss her so much, but she is resting peacefully now.

Lo, children are there in heritance from the Lord: and the fruit of the womb is his reward. **Psalms 127:3**

EIGHT

Like Sisters

A man that hath friends must shew himself friendly: and there is a friend that sticketh closer than a brother.
Proverbs 18:24

This is so amazing to recapture a lifetime friendship on paper. If I recapture correctly, I may have been about five and my best friend Renee was four years old. The reason I think it was about that time is because I was getting ready to start school, and I had moved back with my mother.

My youth was filled with many happy days. One lifetime friend was Renee. Renee is a successful attorney in Atlanta with a beautiful family who also practices law. I have so many fond memories of Renee and our friendship as little girls. One of the first memories is when her mother brought her baby brother home from the hospital. We were on the front porch. We lived right next door to one another, and we shared the same porch. As we sat there, we could hear the baby crying. When we got a chance to see the new baby, Renee tells her mother, "His name is going to be Timmy." Her mother replied and said that she had already named him. Everyone did come to call him Timmy (as a nickname).

Another great story which includes a day while playing outside when we got hungry. Renee went into the house to get all the children a snack. The only thing she could find was a pack of wieners. We were easy to please as the kids. We each took one as she began to pass out the uncooked wieners. That's right, we ate them right out the pack and they were so good. Well, the story doesn't end there. Her mother began to look for the wieners because she was going to make pork and beans with wieners for dinner. While you're reading this, I need you to find the humor in this story because I am absolutely laughing within myself as I am remembering that day and how hilarious it was. Her mother came through the back door to my mother's apartment and tells her that her wieners are missing. At that point, all the other children left the backyard to eat their wieners without conviction. My mother began to help her mother search for the missing wieners. The funny thing is, the two of us had not finished our wieners. We were still eating when our mother's notice what was in our hands. We were not very good in hiding things because we still had the empty package with us too. We had no idea we had done anything wrong. Not sure what they had for dinner that night.

This story includes the baby Timmy. Here we are again as children looking for some snacks. If I learned anything from being a child and wanting snacks was how to provide snacks for my own children. This was a true-life lesson. This story is more hilarious than the previous one. Again, we were in the yard playing. Renee went in the house and brought out some chocolate candy. It looked like a chocolate bar we had eaten before. I don't know about you but as for me yes, I wanted a piece of the chocolate candy. We divided the pack, of course we gave the baby a small piece of the chocolate too. Now here we go again as we watch her mother panic because the baby had an upset stomach. My mother begin to assist her mother with the baby. Renee and I begin to run to the restroom. The walls were so thin in the apartment that when we would go to the restroom, we could talk to each other while sitting in our own apartment. At some point her mother realized that there was an empty box of ex-lax. They noticed the two of us continually going into the restroom. I'm sure Mrs. Anne had mixed emotions once she realized we had fed her baby ex-lax and felt relieved that there was nothing wrong with her baby. As usually the laxative had to run its course through the baby just like it had to do with Renee and me. Can you imagine a baby with cloth diapers in that situation?

One other funny stories is about going with Renee's mother to the department store in the community called Atlantic Mills. She was my mother's best friend. She would take her children and me with her when she go shopping. The store was only about two or three blocks from our apartment. One of the highlights of going to that department store was getting a snow cone. As we walk back home, we were trying to see if we could get all the juice out of the snow cone before we got there. When we got back to the apartment my mother looked at me and asked her friend what happened to Sherry's lips. My lips had swollen from staying on the ice for a long period of time. Now, as an adult I'm sensitive to direct sunlight.

Another story that happened while playing with my "like" sister and her brothers was an instance where we had been to a birthday party, and we had birthday toys. Well, her brothers took the whistle out of the toy and begin to just use it to make sounds. So, Renee and I decided to take ours out of the toy and begin to make the sounds too. As life would have it, I swallowed mine. Her mother was a health professional, and they noticed me changing colors in my face and struggling to breathe. The two women (our mothers) began to pick me up and turn me upside down while beating my back until the item came from within my throat. My question when they retrieved the foreign object from my throat was, could I have my toy back? Now I see why God gave us mothers, because a child like me needed two mothers to keep me safe.

I can reflect on how we used to walk home from downtown instead of riding the bus. When we walked with Renee's brothers (Anthony, Charles, and Glenn), we would stop at the funeral homes that was in the Civil Right district to get a cool sip of water from their water fountain. The funeral homes were black owned. We appreciated and respected their courtesy. That was so unique because nobody ever stopped us at the door and said no trespassing. Both funeral homes were in what we now call the Civil Rights area. It was a safe place for us to stop to refresh ourselves. There were other businesses in that neighborhood such as a doctor who lived in part of his house and his office was in the other part. The house was very big, well-kept, and respected by the community. There was a boy's club in the neighborhood also and Renee's brothers attend there regularly. That area was a prosperous area for black businesses in that neighborhood. I'm glad I got a chance to witness that beautiful community before it changed. Closer to our apartment is where we witness the new construction of the new freeway. I am thankful for being able to witness all those life changing experiences.

As time went on, our mothers found larger apartments on different sides of town in Birmingham. Renee went to a different elementary school. Our mothers stayed best friends so there was always a connection for us. Renee has brothers which ended up being like my brothers. For years we told people we were sisters then we begin to tell them we were cousins but today I can gladly say we are like sisters. We have a friendship and a bond that is irreplaceable in our heart.

There are so many other great stories. One thing we always must remember about true friendship is, that whether we see one another every day or talk to one another every day or not, our friendship has been bonded by love and it can't be taken away by absence or distance.

Beloved, let us love one another: for love is of God; and everyone that loveth is born of God, and knoweth God. **1 John 4:7**

NINE

Remembering Mother

Honour thy father and mother: which is the first commandment with promise. **Ephesian 6:2**

Having precious memories of my mother is always a great way to start my day.

This morning, from my reflection I saw my mother in the mirror. The memories of her sweet face lingered in my mind.

As prepared breakfast, I recognized the alluring coffee aroma and the sweet smell of toast coming from my kitchen. Yes, my mother's favorite breakfast was in my kitchen. It didn't frighten me because it was such a sweet gentle remembrance.

Later that day, I looked at a video that one of my classmates posted on social media and I saw my mother smile on my face. She liked to throw her head back when she laughed and so do I.

My oldest living niece Cynthia came by to visit me, and she looked at my hair which was longer at the time, and she said you have hair just like big mommas. Amazingly my hair will grow longer in the back just like my mother's hair.

Wednesdays was her off day from work, and she would always make a great home cooked meal just like she did on Sunday. Yes, now some Wednesdays and Sundays are my special meal days.

Surprisingly, on Saturdays I wax the hardwood floors and making sure the dusting is done just as I was learned to do as a child before I could watch cartoons. Only difference is, I do not use the paste wax or watch cartoons.

There are lots of things that I learned from her as a child. I could not speak about certain things, and I knew when to keep quiet. She knew about a lot of things, but she would not say anything until the time was right to speak. Secrets that she shared with me I have never told them. I think that's why so many people can trust me because I will make the promise and I must keep it. I learned from my mother that the best kept secret is the one you do not tell.

I never realized that the things she was teaching me would be life lessons that I would use when I got older.

Children, obey your parents in the Lord: for this is right.
Ephesians 6:1

Tributes to the Author

To the greatest mom in the world! You are an inspiration to the whole world, but your strength, grace and wisdom has been my motivation and has molded me into the woman I have become. Thank you for choosing to nurture me and love me unconditionally. I am forever grateful and sometimes in awe that such an amazing woman is my mom. Continue to share the gift God has given you and thank you for passing the torch of greatness and creating a great legacy for me, my siblings, my cousins, and the next generations.

Love you,

---Toy, Daughter

Congratulations on your new writing experience! You are the example of a hard-working, multitalented, and dedicated individual. Everything you touched has blossomed and bloomed into a beautiful flower garden. Please continue to be all that God has called you to be, because your offspring are watching and wanting to be just like you. Blessings and love to you, forever and always!

---Derrick, Tamara, Chloe and Carmen:
Daughter and Family

You are a jewel to me and the family. Smart, well-rounded, and always had my attention with a great story to tell. A great educator in words and deeds! First cousin, and also one of my very best friends. Continue to be great my dear cousin!

--Gwen, Cousin

Aunt Sherry is the best. She has a great heart and loves her family. She has all these great memories about our family. Some of these people I haven't even seen but to hear her talk about them, I would love to have met them.

--- Cynthia, Niece

My friend Sherry is a quiet yet talented woman of God. She exhibits her faith daily, through her work and kindness to others. I have seen this manifested in both the work force and in her personal life. She never misses an opportunity to share her love for where she grew up and the community, for which she came from. Her pride and resilience are written all over her face when she tells of her upbringing. Anyone who meets her is drawn to her as an inspiration and role model.

--- Brenda, Retired Education Administrator

Go Auntie! I truly admire your tenacity and courage. I am grateful that you are my Auntie.

--- Shawn, Nephew

"Because of the Lord's great love, we are not consumed, for His compassions never fail. They are new every morning, great is your faithfulness. "- Lamentations 3:22-23

I am so excited about what God is doing in the life of my friend, Sherry. I encourage everyone to read her book. Sherry is confident, compassionate, and courageous. She is reminding us to enjoy the unique, wonderful, and destiny-filled life God has given us. Although we know God is ever-present and faithful, we are still sometimes overwhelmed by life. Sherry's book talks about her real-life issues.

--- Erma, Retired Educator

Congratulations, Amen, and Thank you for expanding on the lineage of our family. The Family now is now history by your written works.

--- Shana, Niece

My friend Sherry is a determined, empowered woman who is successful in her career and family life. Sherry stands for what/who she believes in. Sherry has faced many challenges, but managed to rise to the TOP, she is a dear friend of which I am pleased and proud to say "Bravo, you go my President".

--- Charlene, Educator, Former V.P.

I met Sherry 20 year ago. To know her is to respect her as woman. I love her as an individual and to honor her in all her greatness, accomplishment, and achievements.

Sherry played a tremendous part and unmatched involvement and encouragement with my five children in the public school system, here in Alabama. All my children have graduated with honors with her studious involvement, encouragement, and guidance. I'm Also Sherry's Stylist. I'm most humbly proud of her. She could've chosen several stylists, but she chose to support me and for that I'm grateful. Sherry is nothing short of a phenomenal woman inside and out, and my family love her dearly.

--- Theresa, Parent/Hairstylist

Friends are important part of everyone's life. A friend is someone with whom you can share your celebrations, disappointments. dreams, concerns. and who will be there to support you in times of uncertainty. I have many friends, but Sherry is a special but rare kind of friend. I met Sherry many years ago at the NEA 153rd Representative Assembly in Orlando Florida. Our friendship began at that conference as we talked about issues that affect education such as the advancement of equitable and quality public education in Alabama. As the conference was ending on that Saturday evening, we exchanged telephone numbers and called each other regularly. Also, we attended various conferences such as Leadership Conference, Minority Leadership Training Conference, and Delegate Assembly. My two memorable events about Sherry were when she called me and said that she was running for leadership office and when she surprised me by coming to Huntsville, Alabama in May of 2016 and sworn me in as local President. These two defining events I will always cherish and remember. Sherry not only as a friend but a true sister in Christ. I will be always love her for supporting and encouraging me on my leadership journey.

A True Friend for Life.

--- Deborah, Retired Educator/Leader

Sherry, President, Mom, Friend, these are the titles I know the author by, and I am so honored to be able to share these words with you. I met Ms. Sherry at a Minority Leadership Training (MLT) Conference at Peridio Beach, Alabama. She was the contact for registering her local association for the conference on site, I was impressed with her professionalism and how smoothly she handled the process. Later, in the conference, Ms. Sherry surprised me with a slice of pecan pie, and this became the beginning of a budding friendship. We became friends and at every MLT conference, I knew I would see her, and she would always have a slice of pecan pie for me. I did not know then that later she would be the President and I would work directly with her as her Administrative Assistant. *One often hears the phrase, "God works in mysterious ways", He does.* Ms. Sherry served two consecutive terms as the making history as the first Black Education Support President of the Association and the first President to succeed herself. This is no small accomplishment. Sherry is a champion for education, family, friends, and anyone who needs help; she helps and encourages others to help also. Sherry works hard and she expects others to work hard. She is humble, personable and my friend.

Respectfully,

--Monica, Former Administrative Assistant